First published in the United Kingdom in 2018 by Lantana Publishing Ltd., London
www.lantanapublishing.com

Hardback ISBN: 978-1-911373-65-0
Paperback ISBN: 978-1-911373-32-2

A CIP catalogue record for this book is available from the British Library.

Printed and bound in Europe
Original artwork created digitally

With thanks to Farrah Serroukh, Nicky Parker and Sarah Shannon

PEACE AND ME

Ali Winter . Mickaël El Fathi

LANTANA PUBLISHING

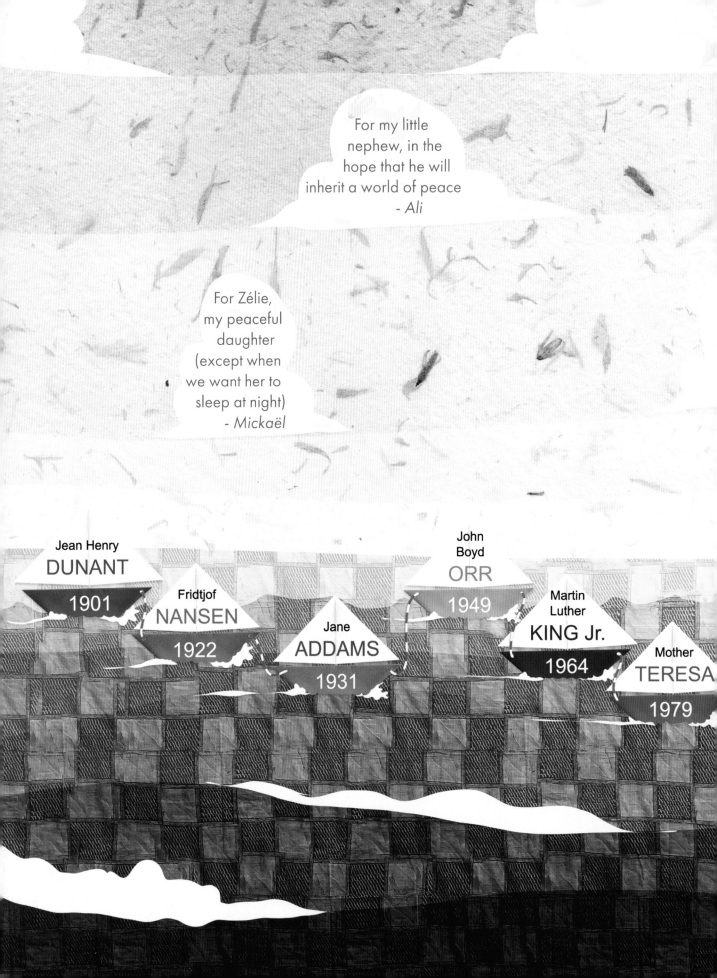

ALFRED NOBEL and the Nobel Prize

ALFRED NOBEL invented a substance that helped countries go to war, but he is best remembered for his amazing contribution to world peace. How did this happen?

As an ambitious young man from Sweden, Alfred moved to Paris in the 1840s to study chemical engineering. There he met an Italian chemist who had invented a liquid called nitroglycerin that exploded when it got hot.

Experiments with this dangerous liquid had killed and injured several people. Alfred was determined to make it safe to use. He did lots of experiments until he found a way to turn the liquid into a solid form that could be blown up safely. He called his invention dynamite.

Dynamite sold like hot cakes! It could blast through rock and was used in building projects all over the world. Alfred built over ninety factories in twenty countries and became a very rich man. But all his newfound wealth didn't make him happy. He realised that his invention was also being used as a weapon of war, and this worried him a great deal.

But then he had an idea.

When Alfred died, he left behind a set of instructions in his will. The money he had made would be given out as prizes each year to the person who had achieved something of "greatest benefit to mankind". The prizes would be in Physics, Chemistry, Medicine, Literature and Peace.

It is this final prize that has inspired this book. Turn the page to discover some of the amazing men and women who have been awarded the Nobel Peace Prize, and the inspirational peace ideas they have left behind...

Alfred Nobel was born in 1833 and died in 1896. The first Nobel Peace Prize was awarded in 1901.

Peace is...helping those in trouble

Inspired by the life of Jean Henry Dunant

JEAN HENRY DUNANT was born in Geneva, Switzerland, into a wealthy family that cared for the poor.

When he was thirty-one, he thought of a plan to make his fortune and went to meet the French president Napoleon III to ask for his help. Napoleon was in a small Italian town called Solferino, leading his army in a battle against Austrian troops.

When Jean arrived, there were thousands of wounded and dying soldiers lying among the dead on the battlefield. He was horrified. He forgot his own money-making ideas and set about helping the soldiers.

He set up a hospital inside a local church and bought supplies to help the wounded. He asked women in the town to nurse the injured from both sides of the battle—friend or foe. His motto was *Tutti Fratelli*, which means *All Are Brothers*.

When Jean returned home, he wrote a book about his experiences. He had an idea that an organisation should be set up to care for wounded soldiers, whichever side of the battle they were on. Many important people read his book and were impressed by his ideas.

In the years that followed, an international organisation was formed to help people in crisis. It was named the Red Cross. Over a hundred years later, wherever there is conflict or disaster, the Red Cross can still be found.

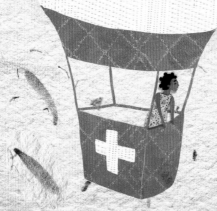

Jean Henry Dunant
(1828-1910) won the Nobel
Peace Prize in 1901

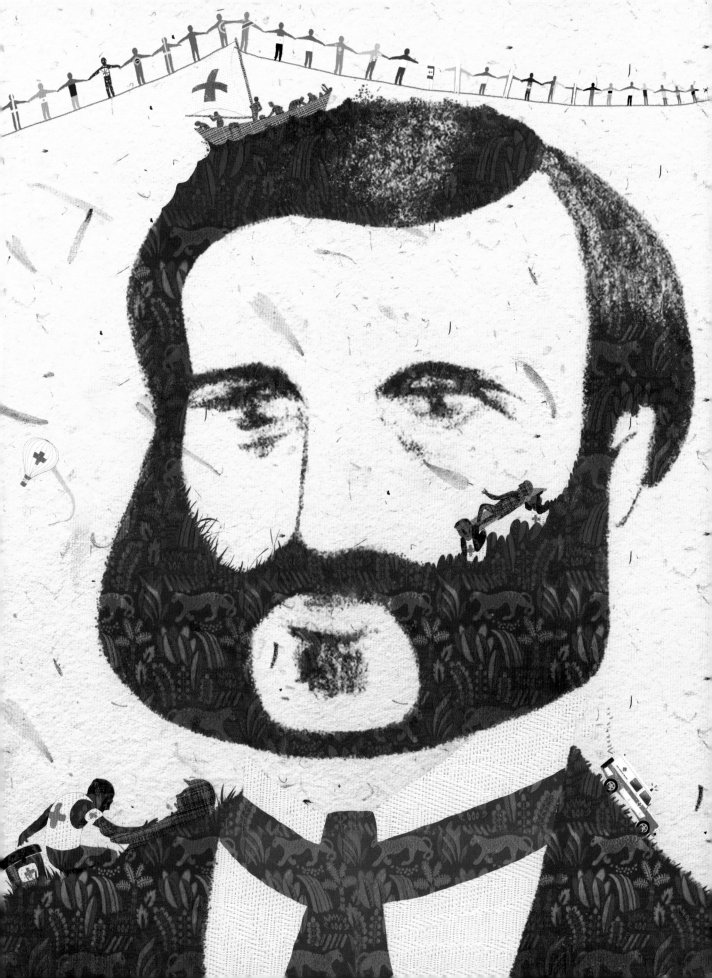

Peace is...
making sure everyone has a home

As a child, FRIDTJOF NANSEN loved spending time outdoors and camping in the forest near his home in Norway. He was so good at sport that he broke the world speed skating record when he was only eighteen years old.

Fridtjof decided to study zoology at university because he thought this subject would keep him outdoors rather than in stuffy lecture halls. Soon he was invited to join a ship sailing to Greenland. The voyage lasted many months and sparked a lifelong spirit of adventure.

From then on, Fridtjof set sail whenever he could. He led a team across Greenland on cross-country skis, and came closer to the North Pole than any other person before him. He had become the most famous explorer in the world!

After World War I, the newly-formed League of Nations asked Fridtjof to help nearly half a million prisoners of war make their way home. The skills he had learned from his years of exploring made his efforts a success. Next, he turned his sights to finding homes for several million refugees.

One of the biggest hurdles Fridtjof faced was that many refugees lacked identity papers to prove their nationality. He invented the "Nansen passport", a certificate that allowed them to travel freely across borders between countries. It was approved by over fifty governments.

The great explorer who was always leaving home to travel the world became even more famous for helping refugees find homes of their own.

Fridtjof Nansen (1861-1930) won the Nobel Peace Prize in 1922

Inspired by the life of Fridtjof Nansen

Peace is...giving people the skills to thrive
Inspired by the life of Jane Addams

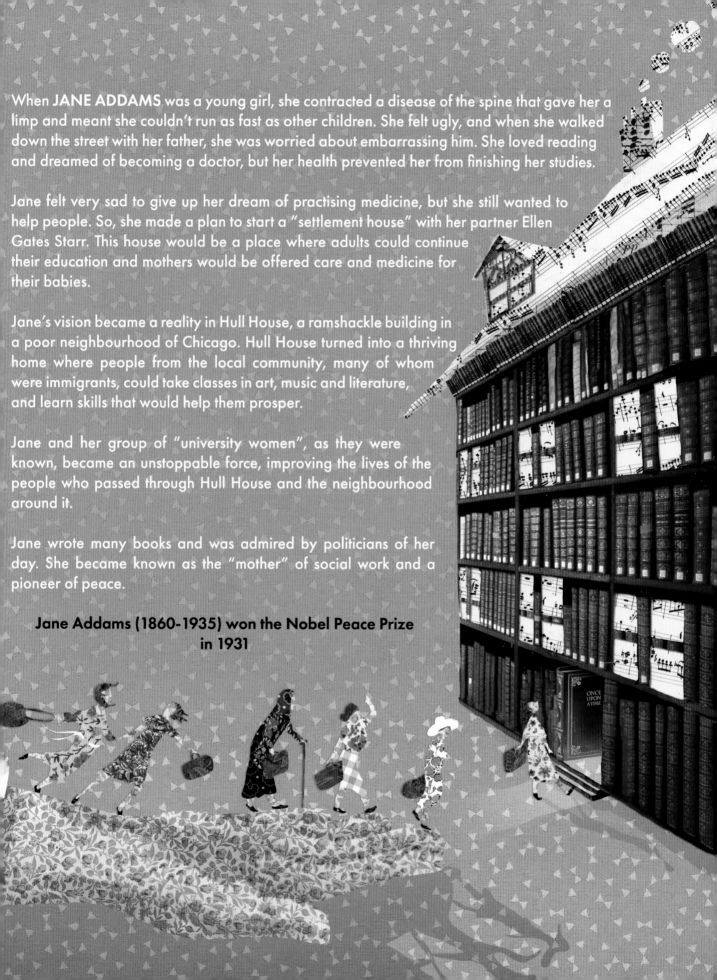

When **JANE ADDAMS** was a young girl, she contracted a disease of the spine that gave her a limp and meant she couldn't run as fast as other children. She felt ugly, and when she walked down the street with her father, she was worried about embarrassing him. She loved reading and dreamed of becoming a doctor, but her health prevented her from finishing her studies.

Jane felt very sad to give up her dream of practising medicine, but she still wanted to help people. So, she made a plan to start a "settlement house" with her partner Ellen Gates Starr. This house would be a place where adults could continue their education and mothers would be offered care and medicine for their babies.

Jane's vision became a reality in Hull House, a ramshackle building in a poor neighbourhood of Chicago. Hull House turned into a thriving home where people from the local community, many of whom were immigrants, could take classes in art, music and literature, and learn skills that would help them prosper.

Jane and her group of "university women", as they were known, became an unstoppable force, improving the lives of the people who passed through Hull House and the neighbourhood around it.

Jane wrote many books and was admired by politicians of her day. She became known as the "mother" of social work and a pioneer of peace.

Jane Addams (1860-1935) won the Nobel Peace Prize in 1931

Peace is...making sure no one goes hungry

Inspired by the life of John Boyd Orr of Brechin

JOHN BOYD ORR was born in a small village in Scotland and grew up to be a teacher. He noticed that lots of his poorer pupils couldn't concentrate in class because they were hungry. This observation stayed with him and, after a few years, he left teaching and went back to university to study biology and medicine.

During World War I, John used his skills as a surgeon to treat wounded soldiers and won medals for his bravery. He gave his men fruit and vegetables from the deserted fields and gardens they marched through, and his soldiers became the healthiest in the army.

When the war was over, John returned to Scotland to continue learning about better diets. He found that giving children milk to drink made them healthier and helped them grow taller. Decades later, many children still receive free milk at school because of his research.

During World War II, John was asked to advise the British government on food. Britain was suffering severe food shortages but John's clever planning meant that many women and children were healthier at the end of the war than they were at the start.

One of the unsung heroes of the war effort, John Boyd Orr helped millions of people avoid starvation during the conflict and in the difficult years that followed.

John Boyd Orr (1880-1971) won the Nobel Peace Prize in 1949

Peace is...treating all people as equals

Inspired by the life of Martin Luther King Jr.

MARTIN LUTHER KING JR. grew up in Atlanta, Georgia. When he was six years old, he was told that he couldn't go to school with the white children he liked to play with in the street. Their school was for white children, and his school was for black children.

Slavery had ended, but there were still rules that separated people by the colour of their skin. Black people didn't just go to separate schools, they also had separate libraries and even separate water fountains.

When Martin grew older, he became a Baptist minister. He heard about Rosa Parks, a brave black woman in Alabama who was arrested when she refused to give up her seat on the bus to a white man. Martin led a boycott against the bus company that lasted over a year. Eventually, the courts decided that the bus company should end segregation on public buses.

Martin had become famous for his role in the bus boycott. His call for peaceful protest in the campaign for racial equality made him the voice of the civil rights movement.

Martin's best-known speech persuaded the government of the United States to make changes to its laws. In this speech, he said, "I have a dream that my four little children will one day live in a nation where they will not be judged by the colour of their skin but by the content of their character".

At the age of thirty-nine, Martin was assassinated. Forty years later, when Barack Obama became America's first African American president, he paid tribute to the bravery and courage of Martin Luther King Jr., who had sacrificed his life for a brighter future.

Martin Luther King Jr. (1929-1968) won the Nobel Peace Prize in 1964

Peace is...
caring for those who are less fortunate

Inspired by the life of Mother Teresa

MOTHER TERESA was born in the city of Skopje in eastern Europe, and her parents named her Agnes. When she was only a girl, she decided to devote her life to the Catholic Church and to helping the poor.

At eighteen, she bravely left her family and travelled to a convent in Ireland where she learned to speak English. After a few months' practice, Sister Teresa, as she had renamed herself, set sail for India.

Sister Teresa became a teacher and was loved by her students, but she was saddened by the poverty around her. She moved out of her Calcutta convent to live among the local people. Wearing a simple white cotton sari with three blue stripes, she found ways to offer love and support to those who needed it, particularly the homeless children whom she loved like a mother.

Sister Teresa became known as Mother Teresa and the Pope permitted her to set up an organisation of nuns who would live among the poor. In this organisation, called the Missionaries of Charity, the nuns would care for "all those people who feel unwanted". Her organisation grew from a handful of women to thousands of volunteers around the world.

The woman who had waved goodbye to her family when she was only a teenager gained a global family by spreading her message of love. After she died, Mother Teresa was declared a saint by the Catholic Church.

Mother Teresa (1910-1997) won the Nobel Peace Prize in 1979

Peace is...finding ways to forgive

Inspired by the life of Desmond Tutu

DESMOND MPILO TUTU was born in a gold-mining town in South Africa and moved with his family to Johannesburg when he was still a boy. His family was not rich, and Desmond earned pocket money by selling peanuts at railway stations.

Desmond earned a place at medical school but his parents couldn't afford the fees, so he accepted a scholarship to study teaching. He was an inspiring teacher but became frustrated by an education system that helped white pupils get ahead in life and held black pupils back.

Desmond decided to study theology and became an Anglican minister. After travelling abroad to study some more, he became the first black Dean of Johannesburg. He went on to become Bishop of Lesotho, Bishop of Johannesburg and Archbishop of Cape Town—the first black minister in each position. He used his achievements to speak out bravely against the South African political system, known as apartheid, that treated black people as second-class citizens.

When Nelson Mandela came to power, Desmond encouraged those who had committed violence during apartheid to apologise to their victims and their victims' families in the hope of forgiveness. It was a revolutionary approach by an extraordinary man and contributed greatly to peace in South Africa.

Desmond Tutu (1931-) won the Nobel Peace Prize in 1984

Peace is...respecting all communities

Inspired by the life of Rigoberta Menchú Tum

When **RIGOBERTA MENCHÚ TUM** was eight years old, she was sent to work in the fields to harvest coffee, sugarcane and cotton. She came from a family of Mayan peasants in Guatemala. Although they were very poor, Rigoberta's mother taught her to be proud of her ancient Mayan heritage.

At that time, a brutal civil war was raging in Guatemala that destroyed hundreds of villages and made a million people homeless. Rigoberta stood by helpless as her father, mother and brother were all killed by the Guatemalan army for opposing the government.

While her sisters escaped into the mountains, Rigoberta stayed in the countryside to campaign for political change. She taught herself Spanish and a number of Mayan languages so that she could pass on her message of resistance to her fellow peasant workers.

At the age of twenty-one, she was forced to flee from Guatemala and seek safety in Mexico. From there she travelled the world speaking out against the oppression of indigenous peoples, and particularly women, in Guatemala and other countries.

She became known for her fearless voice, calling out for respect and fair treatment, and inspiring men and women around the world to do the same.

Rigoberta Menchú Tum (1959-) won the Nobel Peace Prize in 1992

Peace is...valuing the things we have in common

Inspired by the life of Nelson Mandela

ROLIHLAHLA MANDELA was born into the Tembu tribe of the Xhosa people in South Africa. At school, he was given the English name "Nelson", which was easier for white people to say.

When Nelson was expelled from university for joining a protest, he travelled to Johannesburg. There he joined a political party that opposed apartheid. Apartheid was a legal system imposed by the white government based on the colour of people's skin. It took away the rights of black citizens and gave white citizens unfair advantages.

Nelson began to promote armed resistance against the government. He was arrested and sent to prison for almost thirty years. At his trial, he made a speech calling for racial equality and finished with the famous words, "It is an ideal for which I am prepared to die".

All around the world, people called for Nelson to be freed from his prison on Robben Island. When he was finally released, he had so much support that he was elected president of South Africa. He worked tirelessly to unite the black and white citizens of his country through peaceful means, and never tried to take revenge on the people who had put him in prison.

For his determination to mend the deep rifts in his country, Nelson Mandela was heralded as a truly inspirational leader.

Nelson Mandela (1918-2013) won the Nobel Peace Prize in 1993

Peace is...letting silenced voices be heard

SHIRIN EBADI was born in Iran to a well-educated family. From a young age, she had a keen interest in the law and worked hard to receive a law degree before becoming Iran's first-ever female judge.

All this was to change after the Islamic Revolution. The new government said that women could not be judges and Shirin was forced to give up her job and become a clerk in the same courts she had once ruled over. She resigned in protest and sought instead to become a lawyer. For many years her application was refused, but finally she was given permission.

Shirin set up her own law firm and never shied away from difficult cases. She represented the families of murder victims and fought for the freedom of political prisoners. She spoke up for the rights of women and children even when others wouldn't. And she often didn't charge any fees.

One day, while attending a conference abroad, the government seized everything she owned and threatened her with prison if she returned to Iran. Shirin made the difficult decision to stay abroad, not because she was afraid of prison, but because she knew that she wouldn't be able to continue speaking out against oppression if she was behind bars.

Shirin Ebadi has inspired people around the world by bravely standing up for the rights of those whose voices have been silenced, even at great personal cost to herself.

Shirin Ebadi (1947-)
won the Nobel Peace
Prize in 2003.

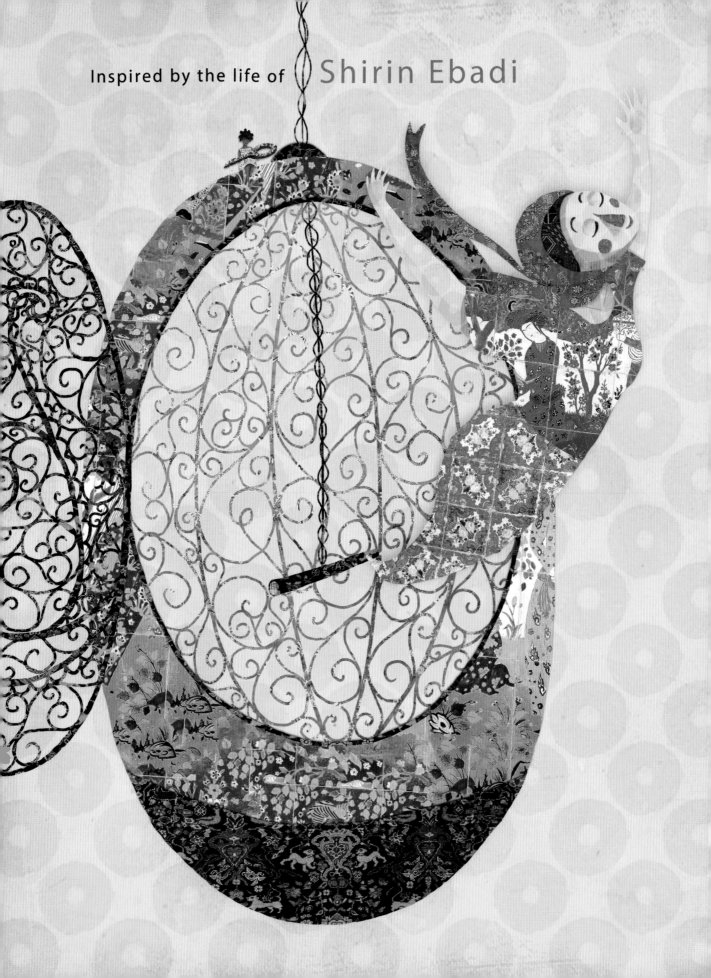

Inspired by the life of Shirin Ebadi

Peace is...
protecting our environment

Inspired by the life of Wangari Maathai

WANGARI MAATHAI grew up in a town in Kenya where children played amongst the trees and a natural spring provided water for the people.

Wangari became the first woman in East and Central Africa to earn a doctorate degree. But when she returned to her village after her studies, she was horrified to find that the trees had all been cut down, the spring had run dry and the countryside was turning into a desert.

Wangari decided to plant a group of native trees in her backyard. Then she encouraged other women to start planting trees, and before long thousands of women all over Kenya had come together to plant seedlings, enough for one tree for every person in the country. The women received a small fee for each seedling that grew, which helped them feed their families. This mass tree planting effort became known as the Green Belt Movement.

Wangari's movement believed in democracy and freedom of speech, and she often came into conflict with the government. But she was firm in her belief that planting trees would improve the quality of the soil, increase food production, provide more firewood for cooking, and create jobs. Soon these ideas spread to other African countries and Wangari was celebrated around the world for her work.

And it all started with a single seed.

Wangari Maathai (1940-2011) won the
Nobel Peace Prize in 2004

Peace is...
making sure
every child gets
to go to school

Inspired by the life of Malala Yousafzai

MALALA YOUSAFZAI was born in a valley in Pakistan at the foot of the mountains. Her father promised her an education, but a political group known as the Taliban took control of the valley. The Taliban banned music and television. Worst of all they banned girls from going to school. Life changed a great deal for Malala and her family.

Malala vowed to tell the world what was happening in her small village. At the age of eleven, she started blogging for the BBC using a false name. Soon, newspapers all over the world had picked up her story and, despite the danger it put her in, Malala began to speak publicly about how important it was for girls to have the chance to be educated.

After a few years, the Taliban were forced out of the valley and Malala was overjoyed to go back to school. However, when she was fifteen, a masked gunman from the Taliban boarded her school bus and shot her. She was badly wounded and taken to a hospital in the United Kingdom where she spent many months recovering from the attack.

Since then she has supported the education of girls in countries around the world. Her courage and determination earned her many prizes and awards. She has become a voice of inspiration for young people everywhere and the youngest person ever to win a Nobel prize.

Malala Yousafzai (1997-) won the Nobel Peace Prize in 2014

Martin Luther
KING Jr.
UNITED STATES

Jane
ADDAMS
UNITED STATES

Rigoberta
MENCHÚ TUM
GUATEMALA

John Boyd
ORR
United
Kingdom

Fridtjof
NANSEN
Norway

Jean Henry
DUNANT
Switzerland

Wangari
MAATHAI
Kenya

Desmond
TUTU
South Africa

Nelson
MANDELA
South Africa

Shirin
EBADI
Iran

Malala
YOUSAFZAI
Pakistan

Mother
TERESA
India

PEACE IS...

...helping those in trouble
...making sure everyone has a home
...giving people the skills to thrive
...making sure no one goes hungry
...treating all people as equals
...caring for those who are less fortunate
...finding ways to forgive
...respecting all communities
...valuing the things we have in common
...letting silenced voices be heard
...protecting our environment
...making sure every child gets to go to school

WHAT DOES PEACE MEAN TO YOU?